FIX IT QUICK™

With a MIX

Pictured on the front cover *(clockwise from top):* Santa Fe Fish Fillet with Mango-Cilantro Salsa *(page 90),* Beef in Wine Sauce *(page 72),* Mexican Taco Salad *(page 44)* and South-of-the-Border Rice and Beans *(page 116).*

Pictured on the back cover: Super Chili for a Crowd *(page 124).*

ISBN-13: 978-1-4127-2728-0
ISBN-10: 1-4127-2728-6

Library of Congress Control Number: 2007932075

Manufactured in China.

8 7 6 5 4 3 2 1

Microwave Cooking: Microwave ovens vary in wattage. Use the cooking times as guidelines and check for doneness before adding more time.

Preparation/Cooking Times: Preparation times are based on the approximate amount of time required to assemble the recipe before cooking, baking, chilling or serving. These times include preparation steps such as measuring, chopping and mixing. The fact that some preparations and cooking can be done simultaneously is taken into account. Preparation of optional ingredients and serving suggestions is not included.

table of contents

express lane appetizers

hot french onion dip

1 envelope LIPTON® RECIPE SECRETS® Onion Soup Mix
1 container (16 ounces) sour cream
2 cups shredded Swiss cheese (about 8 ounces), divided
¼ cup HELLMANN'S® or BEST FOODS® Real Mayonnaise

1. Preheat oven to 375°F. In 1-quart casserole, combine soup mix, sour cream, 1¾ cups Swiss cheese and mayonnaise.

2. Bake uncovered, 20 minutes or until heated through. Sprinkle with remaining ¼ cup cheese.

3. Serve, if desired, with sliced French bread or your favorite dippers.

Makes 2 cups dip

hot french onion dip

bite size tacos

  1 pound ground beef
  1 package (1.25 ounces) taco seasoning mix
  ¾ cup water
  2 cups *French's*® French Fried Onions
  ¼ cup chopped fresh cilantro
  32 bite-size round tortilla chips
  ¾ cup sour cream
  1 cup (4 ounces) shredded Cheddar cheese

1. Cook beef in nonstick skillet over medium-high heat 5 minutes or until browned; drain. Stir in taco seasoning mix, water, *1 cup* French Fried Onions and cilantro. Simmer 5 minutes or until flavors are blended, stirring often.

2. Preheat oven to 350°F. Arrange tortilla chips on foil-lined baking sheet. Top with beef mixture, sour cream, remaining onions and cheese.

3. Bake 5 minutes or until cheese is melted and onions are golden.

Makes 8 appetizer servings

Prep Time: 5 minutes
Cook Time: 15 minutes

italian pita chips

  ½ cup (1 stick) butter, melted
  1 package Italian salad dressing mix
  4 pita bread rounds, split into halves

1. Preheat oven to 300°F. Spray large baking sheet with nonstick cooking spray.

2. Combine butter and dressing mix in small bowl. Brush mixture over pita bread halves; place on prepared baking sheet. Bake about 20 minutes or until crispy.

3. Carefully break pitas into pieces. Serve with your favorite dip or spread.

Makes 4 servings

bite size tacos

party stuffed pinwheels

1 envelope LIPTON® RECIPE SECRETS® Savory Herb with Garlic Soup Mix*
1 package (8 ounces) cream cheese, softened
1 cup shredded mozzarella cheese (about 4 ounces)
2 tablespoons milk
1 tablespoon grated Parmesan cheese
2 packages (13.8 ounces each) refrigerated pizza crust dough

Also terrific with LIPTON® RECIPE SECRETS® Onion Soup Mix.

1. Preheat oven to 425°F. In medium bowl, combine all ingredients except pizza dough; set aside.

2. Unroll pizza dough, then top evenly with filling. Roll up, starting at longest side, jelly-roll style. Cut each roll into 16 rounds. (If rolled pizza dough is too soft to cut, refrigerate or freeze until firm.)

3. On baking sheet sprayed with nonstick cooking spray, arrange rounds cut side down.

4. Bake uncovered, 13 minutes or until golden brown.

Makes 32 pinwheels

quick tip

Quick-to-fix appetizers don't have to look plain or boring. Dress up a platter of hors d'oeuvres with simple garnishes—they don't take much time but still add the perfect finishing touch. If possible, use one of the flavors in the dish or something that complements the dish as a garnish; sprigs of fresh herbs, green onion tops or red and yellow cherry tomatoes are several options. Lemon and lime wedges or slices and strips of citrus peel are a few additional quick, easy ways to garnish savory dishes.

party stuffed pinwheels

appetizer chicken wings

2½ to 3 pounds (12 to 14) chicken wings
1 cup (8 ounces) fat-free French dressing
½ cup KARO® Light or Dark Corn Syrup
1 package (1.4 ounces) French onion soup, dip and recipe mix
1 tablespoon Worcestershire sauce

Cut tips from wings and discard. Cut wings apart at joints and arrange in 13×9×2-inch baking pan lined with foil.

In medium bowl mix dressing, corn syrup, recipe mix and Worcestershire sauce; pour over wings.

Bake in 350°F oven 1 hour, stirring once, or until wings are tender.

Makes 24 servings

Prep Time: 15 minutes
Cook Time: 60 minutes

vegetable hummus

2 cloves garlic
2 cans (15 to 19 ounces each) chick peas or garbanzo beans, rinsed and drained
1 package KNORR® Vegetable recipe mix
½ cup water
½ cup BERTOLLI® Olive Oil
2 tablespoons lemon juice
¼ teaspoon ground cumin
6 (8-inch) whole wheat or white pita breads, cut into wedges

• In food processor, pulse garlic until finely chopped. Add remaining ingredients except pita bread. Process until smooth; chill at least 2 hours.

• Stir hummus before serving. If desired, add 1 to 2 tablespoons additional olive oil, or to taste. Serve with pita wedges.

Makes 3½ cups dip

Prep Time: 10 minutes
Chill Time: 2 hours

appetizer chicken wings

smokey chipotle party dip

¾ **cup sour cream**
¾ **cup mayonnaise**
¾ **cup ORTEGA® Salsa, any variety**
1 **package (1.25 ounces) ORTEGA Smokey Chipotle Taco Seasoning Mix**
   Chopped tomatoes, chopped cilantro, chopped ripe olives and shredded Cheddar cheese
   Blue corn tortilla chips

COMBINE sour cream, mayonnaise, salsa and seasoning mix; stir until blended.

SPREAD dip in shallow serving dish or pie plate and sprinkle with tomatoes, cilantro, olives and cheese. Serve with tortilla chips.   *Makes 2¼ cups dip*

Tip: This flavorful dip is ready to go as soon as you make it, but can also be prepared and refrigerated up to 2 days before serving.

mini cocktail meatballs

1 **envelope LIPTON® RECIPE SECRETS® Onion, Onion Mushroom or Beefy Onion Soup Mix**
1 **pound ground beef**
½ **cup plain dry bread crumbs**
¼ **cup dry red wine or water**
2 **eggs, lightly beaten**

1. Preheat oven to 375°F.

2. In medium bowl, combine all ingredients; shape into 1-inch meatballs.

3. In shallow baking pan, arrange meatballs and bake 18 minutes or until done. Serve, if desired, with assorted mustards or tomato sauce.

Makes about 4 dozen meatballs

smokey chipotle party dip

crispy tortilla chicken

1½ **cups crushed tortilla chips**
1 **package (about 1 ounce) taco seasoning mix**
24 **chicken drummettes (about 2 pounds)**
Salsa (optional)

1. Preheat oven to 350°F. Spray rimmed baking sheet with nonstick cooking spray.

2. Combine tortilla chips and taco seasoning in large shallow bowl. Coat chicken with crumb mixture, turning to coat all sides. Shake off excess crumbs; place chicken on prepared baking sheet.

3. Bake about 40 minutes or until chicken is no longer pink in center. Serve with salsa.   *Makes 2 dozen drummettes*

Variation: This recipe can also be prepared using 1 pound boneless skinless chicken breasts cut into 1-inch strips. Bake at 350°F about 20 minutes or until chicken is no longer pink in center.

baked spinach feta dip

1 **cup HELLMANN'S® or BEST FOODS® Real Mayonnaise**
1 **container (16 ounces) sour cream**
1 **package (10 ounces) frozen chopped spinach, thawed and squeezed dry**
1 **package KNORR® Spring Vegetable recipe mix**
3 **green onions, sliced**
1 **container (4 ounces) feta cheese, crumbled**

1. Preheat oven to 350°F.

2. In 1½-quart casserole, combine all ingredients. Bake 35 minutes or until heated through. Serve with pita chips or in phyllo cups.
                                        Makes about 4 cups dip

Prep Time: 5 minutes
Cook Time: 35 minutes

crispy tortilla chicken

home-style corn cakes

     1 cup yellow cornmeal
     ½ cup all-purpose flour
     ½ teaspoon baking powder
     ½ teaspoon baking soda
     1 envelope LIPTON® RECIPE SECRETS® Onion Soup Mix*
     ¾ cup buttermilk
     1 egg, beaten
     1 can (14¾ ounces) cream-style corn
     2 ounces roasted red peppers, chopped (about ¼ cup)
       I CAN'T BELIEVE IT'S NOT BUTTER!® Spread

Also terrific with LIPTON® RECIPE SECRETS® Golden Onion Soup Mix.

1. In large bowl, combine cornmeal, flour, baking powder and baking soda. Blend soup mix with buttermilk, egg, corn and roasted red peppers; stir into cornmeal mixture.

2. In 12-inch nonstick skillet or on griddle, melt ½ teaspoon I Can't Believe It's Not Butter!® Spread over medium heat. Drop ¼ cup batter for each corn cake and cook, turning once, 5 minutes or until cooked through and golden brown. Remove to serving platter and keep warm. Repeat with remaining batter and additional I Can't Believe It's Not Butter!® Spread if needed. Serve, if desired, with sour cream and prepared salsa.

Makes about 18 corn cakes

Tip: Leftover corn cakes can be wrapped and frozen. Remove them from the wrapping and reheat them straight from the freezer in a preheated 350°F oven for about 15 minutes.

home-style corn cakes

hearty nachos

1 pound ground beef
1 envelope LIPTON® RECIPE SECRETS® Onion Soup Mix
1 can (19 ounces) black beans, rinsed and drained
1 cup salsa
1 package (8½ ounces) plain tortilla chips
1 cup shredded Cheddar cheese (about 4 ounces)

1. In 12-inch nonstick skillet, brown ground beef over medium-high heat; drain.

2. Stir in soup mix, black beans and salsa. Bring to a boil over high heat. Reduce heat to low and simmer 5 minutes or until heated through.

3. Arrange tortilla chips on serving platter. Spread beef mixture over chips; sprinkle with Cheddar cheese. Top, if desired, with sliced green onions, sliced pitted ripe olives, chopped tomato and chopped cilantro.

Makes 8 servings

Prep Time: 10 minutes
Cook Time: 12 minutes

popeye's® classic spinach dip

1 can (13.5 ounces) POPEYE® Spinach
16 ounces sour cream (low-fat may be used)
¾ cup mayonnaise (low-fat may be used)
1 package (1.4 ounces) vegetable soup mix, such as KNORR®
2 cans (8 ounces each) water chestnuts, drained and chopped
3 green onions or 1 small onion, chopped

Drain spinach well. Mix all ingredients until well blended. Cover and chill for several hours before serving. *Makes about 4 cups dip*

Tip: Serve with raw vegetables, chips or crackers, or in a cut-out bread bowl with bread chunks for dipping.

hearty nachos

savory chicken satay

1 envelope LIPTON® RECIPE SECRETS® Onion Soup Mix
¼ cup BERTOLLI® Olive Oil
2 tablespoons firmly packed brown sugar
2 tablespoons SKIPPY® Peanut Butter
1 pound boneless, skinless chicken breasts, pounded and cut into thin strips
12 to 16 large wooden skewers, soaked in water

1. In large plastic bag, combine soup mix, olive oil, brown sugar and peanut butter. Add chicken and toss to coat well. Seal bag and marinate in refrigerator 30 minutes.

2. Remove chicken from marinade, discarding marinade. On skewers, thread chicken, weaving back and forth.

3. Grill or broil skewers until chicken is thoroughly cooked. Serve with your favorite dipping sauces. *Makes 12 to 16 appetizers*

Prep Time: 15 minutes
Marinate Time: 30 minutes
Cook Time: 8 minutes

sausage cheese puffs

1 pound BOB EVANS® Original Recipe Roll Sausage
2½ cups (10 ounces) shredded sharp Cheddar cheese
2 cups biscuit mix
½ cup water
1 teaspoon baking powder

Preheat oven to 350°F. Combine ingredients in large bowl until blended. Shape into 1-inch balls. Place on lightly greased baking sheets. Bake about 25 minutes or until golden brown. Serve hot. Refrigerate leftovers.
Makes about 60 appetizers

savory chicken satay

hot artichoke dip

1 envelope LIPTON® RECIPE SECRETS® Onion Soup Mix*
1 can (14 ounces) artichoke hearts, drained and chopped
1 cup HELLMANN'S® or BEST FOODS® Real Mayonnaise
1 container (8 ounces) sour cream
1 cup shredded Swiss or mozzarella cheese (about 4 ounces)

Also terrific with LIPTON® RECIPE SECRETS® Savory Herb with Garlic, Golden Onion or Onion Mushroom Soup Mix.

1. Preheat oven to 350°F. In 1-quart casserole, combine all ingredients.

2. Bake uncovered, 30 minutes or until heated through.

3. Serve with your favorite dippers.   *Makes 3 cups dip*

Cold Artichoke Dip: Omit Swiss cheese. Stir in, if desired, ¼ cup grated Parmesan cheese. Do not bake.

Prep Time: 5 minutes
Bake Time: 30 minutes

quick tip

*When preparing hot dip for a party, try baking it in two smaller casseroles.
When the first casserole is empty, replace it with the second one,
fresh from the oven.*

hot artichoke dip

sausage pinwheels

2 cups biscuit mix
½ cup milk
¼ cup butter or margarine, melted
1 pound BOB EVANS® Original Recipe Roll Sausage

Combine biscuit mix, milk and butter in large bowl until blended. Refrigerate 30 minutes. Divide dough into two portions. Roll out one portion on floured surface to ⅛-inch-thick rectangle, about 10×7 inches. Spread with half the sausage. Roll lengthwise into long roll. Repeat with remaining dough and sausage. Place rolls in freezer until firm enough to cut easily. Preheat oven to 400°F. Cut rolls into thin slices. Place on *ungreased* baking sheets. Bake 15 minutes or until golden brown. Serve hot. Refrigerate leftovers.

Makes 48 pinwheels

Note: This recipe can be doubled to save some for later. Refreeze after slicing. When ready to serve, thaw slices in refrigerator and bake.

white pizza dip

1 envelope LIPTON® RECIPE SECRETS® Savory Herb with Garlic Soup Mix
1 container (16 ounces) sour cream
1 cup (8 ounces) ricotta cheese
1 cup shredded mozzarella cheese (about 4 ounces), divided
¼ cup (1 ounce) chopped pepperoni (optional)
1 loaf Italian or French bread, sliced

1. Preheat oven to 350°F. In shallow 1-quart casserole, combine soup mix, sour cream, ricotta cheese, ¾ cup mozzarella cheese and pepperoni.

2. Sprinkle with remaining ¼ cup mozzarella cheese.

3. Bake uncovered, 30 minutes or until heated through. Serve with bread.

Makes 3 cups dip

Prep Time: 10 minutes
Bake Time: 30 minutes

sausage pinwheels

salads
in a snap

mexican pasta salad

3 cups (8 ounces) uncooked rotini pasta
1 package (1.25 ounces) ORTEGA® Taco Seasoning Mix
½ cup sour cream
¼ cup water
1 tablespoon vinegar
1 cup cherry tomato halves
1 can (4 ounces) ORTEGA Diced Green Chiles
½ cup diced green bell pepper
1 can (2.25 ounces) sliced olives, drained
2 green onions, sliced
2 ORTEGA Taco Shells, coarsely crushed
½ cup ORTEGA Salsa, any variety
½ cup (2 ounces) shredded Cheddar cheese

COOK pasta according to package directions (do not overcook); drain. Rinse with cold water until cooled; drain.

STIR together taco seasoning mix, sour cream, water and vinegar in large bowl until blended. Stir in pasta, cherry tomatoes, green chiles, bell pepper, olives and green onions.

MICROWAVE crushed taco shells on HIGH (100%) 30 to 45 seconds.

PLACE pasta in serving bowls. Top with salsa, crushed taco shells and cheese just before serving.   *Makes 8 servings*

Tip: Stir in a little more water for a creamier salad.

mexican pasta salad

crunchy layered beef & bean salad

1 pound ground beef or turkey
2 cans (15 to 19 ounces each) black or pinto beans, rinsed and drained
1 can (14½ ounces) stewed tomatoes, undrained
1⅓ cups *French's*® French Fried Onions, divided
1 tablespoon *Frank's*® *RedHot*® Original Cayenne Pepper Sauce
1 package (1¼ ounces) taco seasoning mix
6 cups shredded lettuce
1 cup (4 ounces) shredded Cheddar or Monterey Jack cheese

1. Cook beef in large nonstick skillet over medium heat until thoroughly browned; drain well. Stir in beans, tomatoes, ⅔ cup French Fried Onions, **Frank's RedHot** Sauce and taco seasoning. Heat to boiling. Cook over medium heat 5 minutes, stirring occasionally.

2. Spoon beef mixture over lettuce on serving platter. Top with cheese.

3. Microwave remaining ⅔ *cup* onions 1 minute on HIGH. Sprinkle over salad.
Makes 6 servings

onion-crusted chicken with south of france salad

1 package KNORR® French Onion recipe mix
1 cup plain dry bread crumbs
4 boneless, skinless chicken breast halves (about 1¼ pounds)
⅓ cup HELLMANN'S® or BEST FOODS® Real Mayonnaise
8 cups torn red and/or green leaf lettuce
8 ounces green beans, cooked and chilled
   Goat or feta cheese, crumbled (optional)
   Your favorite WISH-BONE® Vinaigrette Dressing
   Oil-cured olives (for garnish)

Preheat oven to 425°F. Combine Knorr French Onion recipe mix with bread crumbs. Brush chicken with mayonnaise, then coat with bread crumb mixture. Arrange chicken on baking sheet; bake 20 minutes or until thoroughly cooked.

Arrange lettuce, beans and goat cheese on 4 plates. Slice chicken and arrange over lettuce. Drizzle with dressing; garnish with olives. *Makes 4 servings*

crunchy layered beef & bean salad

grilled potato salad

1 envelope LIPTON® RECIPE SECRETS® Onion Soup Mix*
⅓ cup BERTOLLI® Olive Oil
2 tablespoons red wine vinegar
1 clove garlic, finely chopped
2 pounds small red or all-purpose potatoes, cut into 1-inch cubes
1 tablespoon chopped fresh basil leaves *or* 1 teaspoon dried basil leaves,
    crushed
   Freshly ground black pepper

*Also terrific with LIPTON® RECIPE SECRETS® Onion Mushroom or Golden Onion Soup Mix.

1. In large bowl, blend soup mix, oil, vinegar and garlic; stir in potatoes.

2. Grease 30×18-inch sheet of heavy-duty aluminum foil; top with potato mixture. Wrap foil loosely around mixture, sealing edges airtight with double fold. Place on another sheet of 30×18-inch foil; seal edges airtight with double fold in opposite direction.

3. Grill, shaking package occasionally and turning package once, 40 minutes or until potatoes are tender. Spoon into serving bowl and toss with basil and pepper. Serve slightly warm or at room temperature.   *Makes 4 servings*

Oven Method: Preheat oven to 450°F. Prepare foil packet as above. Place in large baking pan on bottom rack and bake, turning packet once, 40 minutes or until potatoes are tender. Toss and serve as above.

grilled potato salad

south-of-the-border salad with creamy lime dressing

Creamy Lime Dressing

⅓ **cup sour cream**
3 **tablespoons chopped cilantro**
2 **tablespoons lime juice**
1 **tablespoon** *each* **vegetable oil and milk**
¼ **teaspoon salt**

Salad

4 **ORTEGA® Taco Shells, crushed**
2 **tablespoons vegetable oil**
1 **pound boneless chicken breasts, cut into strips**
1 **package (1.25 ounces) ORTEGA Taco Seasoning Mix**
¾ **cup water**
1 **package (5 ounces) mixed salad greens**
1 **cup cherry tomato halves**
½ **cup ORTEGA Sliced Jalapeños, coarsely chopped**
½ **cup (2 ounces) shredded Cheddar & Monterey Jack cheese**
1 **avocado, pitted, peeled, sliced and sprinkled with lime juice**

COMBINE all Creamy Lime Dressing ingredients in small bowl; stir until blended.

MICROWAVE crushed taco shells on HIGH (100%) 30 to 45 seconds.

HEAT oil in large skillet over medium-high heat. Add chicken strips; cook and stir 4 to 6 minutes or until chicken is no longer pink. Stir in taco seasoning mix and water. Bring to a boil. Reduce heat to low; cook for 2 to 3 minutes or until mixture is thickened, stirring occasionally. Remove from heat.

COMBINE salad greens, crushed taco shells, tomatoes and jalapeños in large bowl. Divide mixture among four serving plates.

SPRINKLE each salad with cheese; top with chicken strips and avocado slices.

SERVE with Creamy Lime Dressing.   *Makes 4 servings*

south-of-the-border salad with creamy lime dressing

asian shrimp & noodle salad

⅓ cup plus 2 tablespoons vegetable oil, divided
¼ cup cider vinegar
2 tablespoons *French's*® Worcestershire Sauce
2 tablespoons light soy sauce
2 tablespoons honey
1 teaspoon grated fresh ginger *or* ¼ teaspoon ground ginger
2 packages (3 ounces each) chicken-flavor ramen noodle soup
1 pound shrimp, cleaned and deveined with tails left on
2 cups vegetables such as broccoli, carrots and snow peas, cut into
    bite-size pieces
1⅓ cups *French's*® French Fried Onions, divided

1. Combine ⅓ cup oil, vinegar, Worcestershire, soy sauce, honey and ginger until well blended; set aside. Prepare ramen noodles according to package directions for soup; drain and rinse noodles. Place in large serving bowl.

2. Stir-fry shrimp in 1 tablespoon oil in large skillet over medium-high heat, stirring constantly, until shrimp turn pink. Remove shrimp to bowl with noodles. Stir-fry vegetables in remaining oil in skillet over medium-high heat, stirring constantly, until vegetables are crisp-tender.

3. Add vegetable mixture, dressing and *1 cup* French Fried Onions to bowl with noodles; toss to coat well. Serve immediately topped with remaining *⅓ cup* onions. *Makes 6 servings*

Tip: Purchase cut-up vegetables from the salad bar of your local supermarket to save prep time.

Prep Time: 15 minutes
Cook Time: 10 minutes

asian shrimp & noodle salad

tex-mex flank steak salad

½ **pound beef flank steak (about 6 ounces)**
½ **teaspoon Mexican seasoning blend or chili powder**
⅛ **teaspoon salt**
   Olive oil cooking spray
4 **cups mixed salad greens**
1 **can (11 ounces) mandarin orange sections, drained**
2 **tablespoons green taco sauce**

1. Cut flank steak lengthwise in half, then crosswise into thin strips. Combine Mexican seasoning and salt in medium bowl. Add steak strips; toss to coat.

2. Spray large skillet with cooking spray; heat over medium-high heat. Add steak; cook and stir 1 to 2 minutes or until desired doneness.

3. Toss salad greens with orange sections in large bowl. Arrange on serving plates. Top with warm steak; drizzle with taco sauce.   *Makes 2 servings*

wild rice and vegetable salad

1 **package (6.25 ounces) quick-cooking long grain and wild rice mix**
1 **bag (16 ounces) BIRDS EYE® frozen Cauliflower, Carrots and Pea Pods**
⅓ **cup honey Dijon or favorite salad dressing**
2 **green onions, thinly sliced**
¼ **cup sliced almonds**

• Cook rice according to package directions. Transfer to large bowl.

• Cook vegetables according to package directions. Drain; add to rice.

• Stir in dressing, green onions and almonds.

• Serve warm or cover and chill until ready to serve.
                              Makes about 4 side-dish servings

Serving Suggestion: Use this recipe as the base for a variety of main-dish salads, adding smoked chicken or turkey or cooked seafood to the rice and vegetables.

Prep Time: 5 minutes
Cook Time: 15 minutes

tex-mex flank steak salad

refreshing chicken & rice salad

1 package (4.3 ounces) RICE-A-RONI® Long Grain & Wild Rice Pilaf
1 tablespoon vegetable oil
2 cups chopped cooked chicken
2 carrots, sliced lengthwise, cut into slices
1 cucumber, peeled, seeded, cut into short thin strips
½ cup short thin strips red or green bell pepper
2 tablespoons sliced green onions
⅓ cup Italian dressing
    Lettuce

1. Prepare Rice-A-Roni® Mix as package directs, substituting oil for margarine. Cool 10 minutes.

2. In large bowl, combine prepared Rice-A-Roni®, chicken, carrots, cucumber, bell pepper, onions and dressing. Chill 4 hours or overnight. Stir before serving.

3. Serve on lettuce-lined platter.   *Makes 5 servings*

vegetable potato salad

1 envelope LIPTON® RECIPE SECRETS® Vegetable Soup Mix
1 cup HELLMANN'S® or BEST FOODS® Real Mayonnaise
2 teaspoons white vinegar
2 pounds red or all-purpose potatoes, cooked and cut into chunks
¼ cup finely chopped red onion (optional)

1. In large bowl, combine soup mix, mayonnaise and vinegar.

2. Add potatoes and onion; toss well. Chill 2 hours.   *Makes 6 servings*

Prep Time: 20 minutes
Chill Time: 2 hours

refreshing chicken & rice salad

southwestern chicken taco salad

Aluminum foil
Nonstick cooking spray
6 (8-inch) plain or flavored flour tortillas
2 (10-ounce) cans HORMEL® chunk breast of chicken, drained and flaked
1 tablespoon taco seasoning mix
2 tablespoons water
1 (15-ounce) can red kidney beans, drained and rinsed
1 (11-ounce) can whole kernel Mexican corn, drained
6 cups shredded lettuce
1 cup shredded Cheddar cheese
1 tomato, diced
1 avocado, diced
1 cup salsa, drained
½ cup sour cream

Preheat oven to 350°F. Make six 2½-inch balls of foil by slightly crushing six 12×12-inch pieces of foil. Lightly spray one side of each flour tortilla and inside of six 10-ounce custard cups or small baking dishes with nonstick cooking spray. Gently press tortillas, sprayed sides up, into custard cups; folding edges to fit as necessary. Place ball of foil in center of each cup. Place cups on baking sheet. Bake shells 10 minutes; remove from oven and remove foil balls. Return to oven and continue baking an additional 3 to 5 minutes or until shells are crisp and edges are lightly browned. Meanwhile, in skillet, combine chunk chicken, taco seasoning mix and water. Simmer over low heat 3 to 5 minutes. Add beans and corn. Heat until warmed through. Place 1 cup shredded lettuce into each tortilla shell. Fill with meat mixture. Top with cheese, tomato and avocado. In small bowl, combine salsa and sour cream. Drizzle dressing over salad and serve. *Makes 6 servings*

southwestern chicken taco salad

greek isle rice salad

1 (6.8-ounce) package RICE-A-RONI® Beef Flavor
2 tablespoons margarine or butter
8 ounces thick sliced deli roast beef, cut into ½-inch pieces
½ cup chopped red onion
½ cup sliced ripe olives
3 plum tomatoes, seeded and chopped
⅓ cup olive oil
¼ cup lemon juice
2 cloves garlic, crushed
½ teaspoon dried oregano
½ teaspoon ground black pepper
1 medium cucumber, thinly sliced
½ cup (2 ounces) crumbled feta cheese

1. In large skillet over medium heat, sauté rice-vermicelli mix with margarine until vermicelli is golden brown.

2. Slowly stir in 2½ cups water and Special Seasonings; bring to a boil. Reduce heat to low. Simmer 15 to 20 minutes or until rice is tender. Cool completely.

3. In large bowl, combine rice mixture, roast beef, onion, olives and tomatoes; set aside.

4. In small bowl, combine olive oil, lemon juice, garlic, oregano and pepper with wire whisk. Toss rice mixture with dressing. Chill at least 30 minutes. Garnish with cucumber slices and cheese.   *Makes 6 servings*

Prep Time: 15 minutes
Cook Time: 30 minutes

greek isle rice salad

mexican taco salad

1 pound ground beef or turkey
1 cup chopped onion
1 cup ORTEGA® Salsa-Thick & Chunky
¾ cup water
1 package (1.25 ounces) ORTEGA Taco Seasoning Mix
1 can (about 15 ounces) kidney or pinto beans, rinsed and drained
1 can (4 ounces) ORTEGA Diced Green Chiles
3 cups tortilla chips *or* 6 taco shells, broken into large pieces
6 cups shredded lettuce, divided
¾ cup (3 ounces) shredded Nacho & Taco blend cheese, divided

Suggested Toppings
Sour cream, guacamole, ORTEGA Thick & Smooth Taco Sauce

COOK beef and onion in large skillet over medium-high heat until beef is brown; drain. Stir in salsa, water and seasoning mix. Bring to a boil. Reduce heat to low; cook for 2 to 3 minutes. Stir in beans and chiles.

LAYER ingredients as follows on ½ cup chips: 1 cup lettuce, ¾ cup meat mixture, 2 tablespoons cheese and desired toppings.   *Makes 6 servings*

quick tip

To meet USDA standards, all ground beef must be at least 70 percent lean. Ground sirloin is the leanest, containing about 15 percent fat. Ground round is a little fattier, with 20 to 23 percent fat, and ground chuck contains between 23 and 30 percent fat. The label will usually state the percentage of fat or lean, but if it doesn't, you can look at the meat itself—fattier ground beef will be lighter in color.

mexican taco salad

oh-so-easy
soups & stews

shrimp and pepper noodle bowl

2 packages (3 ounces each) shrimp-flavored instant ramen noodle
   soup mix

8 ounces frozen cooked medium shrimp *or* 1 package (8 ounces) frozen
   cooked baby shrimp

1 cup frozen bell pepper strips

¼ cup chopped green onions

1 tablespoon soy sauce

½ teaspoon hot pepper sauce

2 tablespoons chopped cilantro (optional)

1. Bring 4 cups water to a boil in large saucepan over high heat. Remove
seasoning packets from noodles; set aside. Break up ramen noodles; add to
water. Add shrimp and bell pepper; cook 3 minutes.

2. Add seasoning packets, green onions, soy sauce and hot pepper sauce;
cook 1 minute. Garnish with cilantro.   *Makes 4 servings*

shrimp and pepper noodle bowl

black & white mexican bean soup

1 tablespoon vegetable oil
1 cup chopped onion
1 clove garlic, minced
¼ cup flour
1 package (1.25 ounces) ORTEGA® Taco Seasoning Mix
2 cups milk
1 can (about 14 ounces) chicken broth
1 package (16 ounces) frozen corn
1 can (about 15 ounces) great northern beans, rinsed and drained
1 can (about 15 ounces) black beans, rinsed and drained
1 can (4 ounces) ORTEGA Diced Green Chiles
2 tablespoons chopped cilantro

HEAT oil in large pan or Dutch oven over medium-high heat. Add onion and garlic; cook until onion is tender.

STIR in flour and taco seasoning mix; gradually stir in milk until blended. Add remaining ingredients except cilantro.

BRING to a boil, stirring constantly. Reduce heat to low; simmer for 15 minutes or until thickened, stirring occasionally.

STIR in cilantro. *Makes 6 servings*

Tip: To save time, substitute ½ teaspoon bottled minced garlic for garlic clove.

black & white mexican bean soup

oven-baked stew

2 pounds boneless beef chuck or round steak, cut into 1-inch cubes
¼ cup all-purpose flour
1⅓ cups sliced carrots
1 can (14 to 16 ounces) whole peeled tomatoes, undrained and chopped
1 envelope LIPTON® RECIPE SECRETS® Onion Soup Mix*
½ cup dry red wine or water
1 cup fresh or canned sliced mushrooms
1 package (8 ounces) medium or broad egg noodles, cooked and drained

Also terrific with LIPTON® RECIPE SECRETS® Beefy Onion or Onion Mushroom Soup Mix.

1. Preheat oven to 425°F. In 2½-quart shallow casserole, toss beef with flour, then bake uncovered, 20 minutes, stirring once.

2. *Reduce heat to 350°F.* Stir in carrots, tomatoes, soup mix and wine.

3. Bake covered, 1½ hours or until beef is tender. Stir in mushrooms and bake covered, an additional 10 minutes. Serve over hot noodles.

Makes 8 servings

Slow Cooker Method: In slow cooker, toss beef with flour. Add carrots, tomatoes, soup mix and wine. Cook covered, on LOW 8 to 10 hours. Add mushrooms; cook covered, on LOW 30 minutes or until beef is tender. Serve over hot noodles.

Prep Time: 20 minutes
Cook Time: 2 hours

oven-baked stew

chicken gumbo

2 tablespoons all-purpose flour
2 teaspoons blackened seasoning mix or Creole seasoning mix
¾ pound boneless skinless chicken thighs, cut into ¾-inch pieces
1 tablespoon olive oil
1 large onion, coarsely chopped
½ cup sliced celery
2 teaspoons minced garlic
1 can (about 14 ounces) reduced-sodium chicken broth
1 can (14½ ounces) stewed tomatoes, undrained
1 large green bell pepper, cut into chunks
1 teaspoon filé powder (optional)
2 cups hot cooked rice
2 tablespoons chopped fresh parsley

1. Combine flour and blackened seasoning mix in large resealable food storage bag. Add chicken; seal bag. Toss to coat.

2. Heat oil in large deep nonstick skillet or saucepan over medium heat. Add chicken; sprinkle with any remaining flour mixture. Cook and stir 3 minutes. Add onion, celery and garlic; cook and stir 3 minutes.

3. Add broth, tomatoes with liquid and bell pepper; bring to a boil. Reduce heat; cover and simmer 20 minutes or until vegetables are tender. Uncover; simmer 5 to 10 minutes or until liquid is slightly reduced. Remove from heat; stir in filé powder, if desired. Ladle into shallow bowls; top with rice and parsley.   *Makes 4 servings*

Note: Filé powder, made from dried sassafras leaves, thickens and adds flavor to gumbos. Look for it in the herb and spice section of your supermarket. Never add it to gumbo while it's still on the heat, or if you plan to reheat leftovers, because cooking filé powder causes it to become stringy and tough.

Prep Time: 15 minutes
Cook Time: 40 minutes

chicken gumbo

thai noodle soup

1 package (3 ounces) ramen noodles
¾ pound chicken tenders
2 cans (about 14 ounces each) chicken broth
¼ cup shredded carrot
¼ cup frozen snow peas
2 tablespoons thinly sliced green onions
½ teaspoon minced garlic
¼ teaspoon ground ginger
3 tablespoons chopped fresh cilantro
½ lime, cut into 4 wedges

1. Break noodles into pieces. Cook noodles according to package directions; discard flavor packet. Drain; set aside.

2. Cut chicken into ½-inch pieces. Combine chicken broth and chicken in large saucepan or Dutch oven; bring to a boil over medium heat. Cook 2 minutes.

3. Add carrot, snow peas, green onions, garlic and ginger. Reduce heat to low; simmer 3 minutes. Add cooked noodles and cilantro; heat through. Serve soup with lime wedges. *Makes 4 servings*

Prep and Cook Time: 15 minutes

quick tip

When purchasing cilantro, look for bright green leaves with no signs of yellowing or wilting. To keep cilantro fresh longer, place the stem ends in a glass of water (like a bouquet), cover loosely with a plastic bag and refrigerate.

thai noodle soup

southwestern beef stew

1 tablespoon plus 1 teaspoon BERTOLLI® Olive Oil, divided
1½ pounds boneless beef chuck, cut into 1-inch cubes
1 can (4 ounces) chopped green chilies, drained
2 large cloves garlic, finely chopped
1 teaspoon ground cumin (optional)
1 can (14 to 16 ounces) whole or plum tomatoes, undrained and chopped
1 envelope LIPTON® RECIPE SECRETS® Onion or Beefy Onion Soup Mix
1 cup water
1 package (10 ounces) frozen cut okra or green beans, thawed
1 large red or green bell pepper, cut into 1-inch pieces
4 frozen half-ears corn-on-the-cob, thawed and each cut into 3 round
    pieces
2 tablespoons chopped fresh cilantro (optional)

1. In 5-quart Dutch oven or heavy saucepan, heat 1 tablespoon olive oil over medium-high heat and brown half of the beef; remove and set aside. Repeat with remaining beef; remove and set aside.

2. In same Dutch oven, heat remaining 1 teaspoon olive oil over medium heat and cook chilies, garlic and cumin, stirring constantly, 3 minutes. Return beef to Dutch oven. Stir in tomatoes and soup mix blended with water. Bring to a boil over high heat. Reduce heat to low and simmer covered, stirring occasionally, 1 hour.

3. Stir in okra, bell pepper and corn. Bring to a boil over high heat. Reduce heat to low and simmer covered, stirring occasionally, 30 minutes or until meat is tender. Sprinkle with cilantro. *Makes 6 servings*

southwestern beef stew

hearty corn & cheese chowder

  4 thick slices bacon, diced
  ¾ cup chopped onion
  2 cups chicken broth or water
  2 cups milk
  1 (6.2-ounce) package PASTA RONI® Shells & White Cheddar
  1 cup frozen or canned corn, drained
  ½ cup finely diced red bell pepper
  ¼ cup chopped chives or green onions

1. In large saucepan over medium heat, cook bacon 5 minutes. Add onion; cook 5 minutes or until bacon is crisp, stirring occasionally. Remove from saucepan; drain. Set aside.

2. To same saucepan, add chicken broth, milk, pasta, corn and bell pepper; bring to a boil. Reduce heat to medium. Simmer uncovered, 12 minutes or until pasta is tender.

3. Stir in bacon mixture and Special Seasonings. Return to a boil; boil 2 to 3 minutes. Ladle into bowls; top with chives.   *Makes 4 servings*

Prep Time: 10 minutes
Cook Time: 25 minutes

mexicali vegetable soup

   ½ pound ground beef
   ½ cup chopped onion
  3½ cups (two 15-ounce cans) beef broth
   1 can (14½ ounces) small white beans, drained
   1 cup sliced zucchini
   1 cup frozen sliced carrots
   1 package (1.25 ounces) ORTEGA® Taco Seasoning Mix

COOK beef and onion in large saucepan until beef is browned; drain. Add broth, beans, zucchini, carrots and seasoning mix. Bring to a boil. Reduce heat to low; cook, covered, for 15 to 20 minutes.   *Makes 6 to 8 servings*

patrick's irish lamb soup

1 tablespoon olive oil

1 medium onion, coarsely chopped

1½ pounds fresh lean American lamb boneless shoulder, cut into ¾-inch cubes

1 bottle (12 ounces) beer *or* **¾ cup water**

1 teaspoon seasoned pepper

2 cans (14½ ounces each) beef broth

1 package (about 1 ounce) brown gravy mix

3 cups cubed potatoes

2 cups thinly sliced carrots

2 cups shredded green cabbage

⅓ cup chopped fresh parsley (optional)

In 3-quart saucepan with cover, heat oil. Add onion and sauté until brown, stirring occasionally. Add lamb and cook and stir until browned. Stir in beer and pepper. Cover and simmer 30 minutes.

Stir in broth and gravy mix. Add potatoes and carrots; cover and simmer 15 to 20 minutes or until vegetables are tender. Stir in cabbage and cook just until cabbage turns bright green. Garnish with chopped parsley, if desired.

Makes 8 servings

Favorite recipe from **American Lamb Council**

quick hot and sour chicken soup

2 cups chicken broth

2 cups water

1 package (about 10 ounces) refrigerated fully cooked chicken breast strips, cut into pieces

1 package (about 7 ounces) chicken-flavored rice and vermicelli mix

1 large jalapeño pepper,* minced

2 green onions, chopped

1 tablespoon soy sauce

1 tablespoon fresh lime juice

1 tablespoon minced fresh cilantro (optional)

*Jalapeño peppers can sting and irritate the skin, so wear rubber gloves when handling peppers and do not touch your eyes.

1. Combine broth, water, chicken, rice mix, jalapeño, green onions and soy sauce in large saucepan. Bring to a boil over high heat. Reduce heat to low. Cover; simmer 20 minutes or until rice is tender, stirring occasionally.

2. Stir in lime juice; sprinkle with cilantro. *Makes 4 servings*

brunswick stew

12 ounces smoked ham or cooked chicken breast, cut into ¾- to 1-inch cubes

1 cup sliced onion

4½ teaspoons all-purpose flour

1 can (about 14 ounces) stewed tomatoes

2 cups frozen mixed vegetables for soup (such as okra, lima beans, potatoes, celery, corn, carrots, green beans and onions)

1 cup chicken broth

Salt and black pepper

1. Spray large saucepan with nonstick cooking spray; heat over medium heat until hot. Add ham and onion; cook 5 minutes or until ham is browned. Stir in flour; cook over medium to medium-low heat 1 minute, stirring constantly.

2. Stir in tomatoes, mixed vegetables and broth; bring to a boil. Reduce heat to low; simmer, covered, 5 to 8 minutes or until vegetables are tender. Simmer, uncovered, 5 to 8 minutes or until slightly thickened. Season with salt and pepper to taste. *Makes 4 servings*

quick hot and sour chicken soup

southwestern turkey stew

1 tablespoon vegetable oil
1 small onion, finely chopped
1 clove garlic, minced
2 cups chicken broth
2 cups cooked smoked turkey breast, cut into ½-inch pieces
2 cups frozen corn kernels
1 can (about 14 ounces) diced tomatoes
1 package (about 6 ounces) red beans and rice mix
1 to 2 canned chipotle peppers in adobo sauce,* drained and minced
  Chopped green onion (optional)

Canned chipotle peppers can be found in the Mexican section of most supermarkets or gourmet food stores.

1. Heat oil in large nonstick skillet over medium-high heat. Add onion and garlic; cook and stir 3 minutes or until onion is translucent.

2. Add broth; bring to a boil. Stir in turkey, corn, tomatoes, bean mix and chipotle pepper. Reduce heat to low. Cover; cook 10 to 12 minutes or until rice is tender. Let stand 3 minutes. Garnish with green onion.

Makes 4 servings

Substitutions: Use 1 can (about 14 ounces) diced tomatoes with jalapeño peppers *or* ¼ teaspoon chipotle chili powder and 1 minced jalapeño pepper in place of the chipotle peppers.

southwestern turkey stew

bouillabaisse

  2 cups water
  1 package KNORR® Vegetable or Spring Vegetable recipe mix
  1 bottle or can (8 to 10 ounces) clam juice
  2 teaspoons tomato paste
  ½ teaspoon paprika
  ¼ teaspoon saffron threads (optional)
 12 mussels or clams, well scrubbed
1½ pounds mixed seafood (cubed cod, snapper, scallops or shrimp)

• In 3-quart saucepan, bring water, recipe mix, clam juice, tomato paste, paprika and saffron to a boil over medium-high heat, stirring occasionally.

• Add mussels and seafood. Bring to a boil over high heat.

• Reduce heat to low and simmer 5 minutes or until shells open and seafood is cooked through and flakes easily when tested with a fork. Discard any unopened shells.   *Makes 6 servings*

Prep Time: 15 minutes
Cook Time: 10 minutes

cheese ravioli soup

4 cans (20 ounces each) chicken broth
1 package (16 ounces) frozen red pepper stir-fry
4 tablespoons MRS. DASH® Classic Italiano Blend
1 package (13 ounces) frozen mini cheese ravioli
6 tablespoons grated Parmesan cheese

Combine broth, red pepper stir-fry and Classic Italiano Blend in medium saucepan. Bring to a boil. Add ravioli. Simmer 15 to 20 minutes or until ravioli is done. Sprinkle with grated Parmesan cheese.   *Makes 12 servings*

Prep Time: 5 minutes
Cook Time: 20 minutes

bouillabaisse

easy cajun chicken stew

2 tablespoons vegetable oil
1 red bell pepper, diced
1 stalk celery, sliced
1 can (about 14 ounces) diced tomatoes with roasted garlic and onions
1½ cups chicken broth
1 package (about 10 ounces) refrigerated fully cooked chicken breast strips, cut into pieces
1 cup canned kidney beans, rinsed and drained
1 pouch (about 9 ounces) New Orleans-style chicken-flavored ready-to-serve rice mix
¼ teaspoon hot pepper sauce
¼ cup chopped green onions

1. Heat oil in Dutch oven over medium-high heat. Add bell pepper and celery; cook and stir 3 minutes. Add tomatoes and chicken broth; bring to a boil.

2. Add chicken, beans, rice mix and pepper sauce. Reduce heat to low. Cover; cook 7 minutes. Stir in green onions. Remove from heat. Cover; let stand 2 to 3 minutes to thicken.   *Makes 4 servings*

Tip: If canned diced tomatoes with garlic and onions aren't available, substitute 1 can (about 14 ounces) diced tomatoes; add 1 teaspoon minced garlic and ¼ cup chopped onion to the bell pepper mixture.

easy cajun chicken stew

super chili for a crowd

4 tablespoons oil, divided
2 large onions, chopped
1 tablespoon minced garlic
2 pounds boneless top round or sirloin steak, cut into ½-inch cubes
1 pound ground beef
1 can (28 ounces) crushed tomatoes in purée
1 can (15 to 19 ounces) red kidney beans, undrained
¾ cup water
⅓ cup *Frank's® RedHot®* Original Cayenne Pepper Sauce
2 packages (1¼ ounces each) chili seasoning mix

1. Heat 1 tablespoon oil in 5-quart saucepot or Dutch oven until hot. Sauté onions and garlic until tender; transfer to bowl.

2. Heat remaining oil in same pot; cook meat in batches until well browned. Drain fat.

3. Add remaining ingredients to pot. Stir in onion and garlic. Heat to boiling, stirring. Simmer, partially covered, for 1 hour or until meat is tender, stirring often. Garnish as desired.   *Makes 10 servings*

Prep Time: 15 minutes
Cook Time: 1 hour 15 minutes

super chili for a crowd

30-minute paella

2 tablespoons olive oil
1 package (about 10 ounces) chicken-flavored rice and vermicelli mix
¼ teaspoon red pepper flakes
3½ cups water
1 package (about 10 ounces) refrigerated fully cooked chicken breast strips, cut into pieces
1 package (8 ounces) medium raw shrimp, peeled
1 cup frozen peas
¼ cup diced roasted red pepper

1. Heat oil in large skillet over medium heat. Add rice mix and red pepper flakes; cook and stir 2 minutes or until vermicelli is golden.

2. Add water, chicken, shrimp, peas, roasted red pepper and seasoning packet; bring to a boil. Reduce heat to low. Cover; cook 12 to 15 minutes or until rice is tender, stirring occasionally.   *Makes 6 servings*

grilled garlic chicken

1 envelope LIPTON® RECIPE SECRETS® Savory Herb with Garlic Soup Mix
3 tablespoons BERTOLLI® Olive Oil
4 boneless, skinless chicken breast halves (about 1¼ pounds)

1. In medium bowl, combine soup mix with olive oil.

2. Add chicken; toss to coat.

3. Grill or broil until chicken is thoroughly cooked.   *Makes 4 servings*

30-minute paella

beef in wine sauce

4 pounds boneless beef chuck roast, cut into 1½- to 2-inch cubes
2 tablespoons garlic powder
2 cans (10¾ ounces each) condensed golden mushroom soup, undiluted
1 can (8 ounces) sliced mushrooms, drained
¾ cup dry sherry
1 package (about 1 ounce) dry onion soup mix
1 bag (20 ounces) frozen sliced carrots, thawed

1. Preheat oven to 325°F. Spray heavy 4-quart casserole or Dutch oven with nonstick cooking spray.

2. Sprinkle beef with garlic powder. Place in prepared casserole.

3. Combine canned soup, mushrooms, sherry and dry soup mix in medium bowl. Pour over meat; mix well.

4. Cover; bake 3 hours or until meat is very tender. Add carrots during last 15 minutes of baking. *Makes 6 to 8 servings*

summer vegetable & fish bundles

4 fish fillets (about 1 pound)
1 pound thinly sliced vegetables*
1 envelope LIPTON® RECIPE SECRETS® Savory Herb with Garlic or Golden Onion Soup Mix
½ cup water

Use any combination of the following: thinly sliced mushrooms, zucchini, yellow squash or tomatoes.

On two 18×18-inch pieces heavy-duty aluminum foil, divide fish equally; top with vegetables. Evenly pour savory herb with garlic soup mix blended with water over vegetables. Wrap foil loosely around fillets and vegetables, sealing edges airtight with double fold. Grill or broil seam side up 15 minutes or until fish flakes. *Makes about 4 servings*

Menu Suggestion: Serve over hot cooked rice with Lipton® Iced Tea mixed with a splash of cranberry juice cocktail.

beef in wine sauce

sonoma® pot pie

2 cans (10½ ounces each) chicken gravy
3 cups cooked chicken or turkey chunks
1 package (10 ounces) frozen mixed vegetables
⅔ cup SONOMA® Dried Tomato Bits
1 can (3 ounces drained weight) sliced mushrooms
¼ cup water
1½ teaspoons dried thyme leaves, divided
2¼ cups reduced-fat buttermilk baking mix
¾ cup plus 2 tablespoons lowfat milk

Preheat oven to 450°F. In 3-quart saucepan combine gravy, chicken, vegetables, tomato bits, mushrooms, water and ½ teaspoon thyme. Stir occasionally over medium-low heat until mixture comes to a boil. Meanwhile, in large bowl combine baking mix, milk and remaining 1 teaspoon thyme; mix until just combined. Pour chicken mixture into shallow 2-quart casserole or 9-inch square baking dish. Top with large spoonfuls of dough, making equal-sized mounds. Place casserole on baking sheet and bake about 20 minutes or until chicken mixture is bubbly and topping is golden brown.

Makes 4 to 6 servings

garlic pork chops

6 bone-in pork chops, ¾ inch thick
1 envelope LIPTON® RECIPE SECRETS® Savory Herb with Garlic Soup Mix
2 tablespoons vegetable oil
½ cup hot water

1. Preheat oven to 425°F. In broiler pan, without the rack, arrange chops. Brush both sides of pork chops with soup mix blended with oil.

2. Bake pork chops 25 minutes or until done.

3. Remove pork chops to serving platter. Add hot water to pan and stir, scraping brown bits from bottom of pan. Serve sauce over pork chops.

Makes 4 servings

Prep Time: 5 minutes
Cook Time: 25 minutes

sonoma® pot pie

chicken, asparagus & mushroom bake

1 tablespoon butter

1 tablespoon olive oil

2 boneless skinless chicken breasts (about ½ pound), cut into bite-size pieces

2 cloves garlic, minced

1 cup sliced mushrooms

2 cups sliced asparagus

Black pepper

1 package (about 6 ounces) corn bread stuffing mix

¼ cup dry white wine (optional)

1 can (about 14 ounces) chicken broth

1 can (10¾ ounces) condensed cream of asparagus or cream of chicken soup, undiluted

1. Preheat oven to 350°F. Heat butter and oil in large skillet until butter is melted. Add chicken and garlic; cook and stir about 3 minutes over medium-high heat until chicken is no longer pink. Add mushrooms; cook and stir 2 minutes. Add asparagus; cook and stir about 5 minutes or until asparagus is crisp-tender. Season with pepper to taste.

2. Transfer mixture to 2½-quart casserole or 6 small casseroles. Top with stuffing mix.

3. Add wine to skillet, if desired; cook and stir 1 minute over medium-high heat, scraping up any browned bits from bottom of skillet. Add broth and soup; cook and stir until well blended.

4. Pour broth mixture over stuffing mixture; mix well. Bake, uncovered, about 35 minutes (30 minutes for small casseroles) or until heated through and lightly browned. *Makes 6 servings*

chicken, asparagus & mushroom bake

harvest pot roast with sweet potatoes

1 envelope LIPTON® RECIPE SECRETS® Onion Soup Mix
1½ cups plus 3 tablespoons water, divided
¼ cup soy sauce
2 tablespoons firmly packed dark brown sugar
1 teaspoon ground ginger (optional)
1 (3- to 3½-pound) boneless pot roast (rump, chuck or round)
4 large sweet potatoes, peeled, if desired, and cut into large chunks
2 tablespoons all-purpose flour

1. Preheat oven to 325°F. In Dutch oven or 5-quart heavy ovenproof saucepan, combine soup mix, 1½ cups water, soy sauce, brown sugar and ginger; add roast.

2. Cover and bake 1 hour 45 minutes.

3. Add potatoes and bake covered, an additional 45 minutes or until beef and potatoes are tender.

4. Remove roast and potatoes to serving platter and keep warm; reserve juices.

5. In small cup, with wire whisk, blend remaining 3 tablespoons water and flour. In same Dutch oven, add flour mixture to reserved juices. Bring to a boil over high heat. Boil, stirring occasionally, 2 minutes. Serve with roast and potatoes.   *Makes 6 servings*

Slow Cooker Method: In slow cooker, add potatoes, then roast. Combine soup mix, water, soy sauce, sugar and ginger; pour over roast. Cook covered on LOW 8 to 10 hours or HIGH 4 to 6 hours or until roast is tender. Remove roast and potatoes to serving platter. Blend remaining water with flour and stir into juices in slow cooker. Cook covered on HIGH 15 minutes or until thickened.

harvest pot roast with sweet potatoes

broccoli, turkey and noodle skillet

1 tablespoon butter
1 green bell pepper, chopped
1 cup frozen chopped broccoli, thawed
¼ teaspoon black pepper
1½ cups chicken broth
½ cup milk or half-and-half
2 cups diced cooked turkey breast
1 package (about 4 ounces) chicken and broccoli pasta mix
¼ cup sour cream

1. Melt butter in large nonstick skillet over medium-high heat. Add bell pepper, broccoli and black pepper; cook 5 minutes or until bell pepper is crisp-tender. Add chicken broth and milk; bring to a boil. Stir in turkey and pasta mix.

2. Reduce heat to low; cook 8 to 10 minutes or until noodles are tender. Remove from heat; stir in sour cream. Let stand, uncovered, 5 minutes or until sauce is thickened. *Makes 4 servings*

italian-style chicken and rice

1 tablespoon vegetable oil
4 boneless skinless chicken breasts (about 1 pound)
2 cups chicken broth
1 package (about 6 ounces) chicken-flavored rice mix
½ cup chopped red bell pepper
½ cup frozen peas, thawed
¼ cup Romano cheese

1. Heat oil in large skillet. Add chicken; cook over medium-high heat 10 to 15 minutes or until lightly browned on both sides.

2. Add broth, rice mix, bell pepper and peas; mix well. Bring to a boil. Cover; reduce heat and simmer 10 minutes or until chicken is no longer pink in center. Remove from heat; sprinkle with cheese. Cover; let stand 5 minutes or until liquid is absorbed. *Makes 4 servings*

broccoli, turkey and noodle skillet

hearty bbq beef sandwiches

1 envelope LIPTON® RECIPE SECRETS® Onion Soup Mix
2 cups water
½ cup chili sauce
¼ cup firmly packed light brown sugar
1 (3-pound) boneless chuck roast
8 kaiser rolls or hamburger buns, toasted

1. Preheat oven to 325°F. In Dutch oven or 5-quart heavy ovenproof saucepan, combine soup mix, water, chili sauce and sugar; add roast.

2. Cover and bake 3 hours or until roast is tender.

3. Remove roast; reserve juices. Bring reserved juices to a boil over high heat. Boil 4 minutes.

4. Meanwhile, with fork, shred roast. Stir roast into reserved juices and simmer, stirring frequently, 1 minute. Serve on rolls.   *Makes 8 servings*

saucepot spinach lasagne

1 package KNORR® Leek recipe mix
3 cups water
8 ounces uncooked wide egg noodles (about 6 cups)
1 cup milk
1 package (10 ounces) frozen leaf spinach, thawed
2 cups shredded mozzarella cheese, divided (about 8 ounces)
⅓ cup grated Parmesan cheese

• In 4-quart saucepot, combine recipe mix and water. Add noodles and milk. Stirring frequently, heat to boiling. Reduce heat; stirring occasionally, simmer 5 minutes.

• Add spinach; heat to simmering. Stir in 1 cup mozzarella and Parmesan cheese. Spoon into shallow serving bowl and sprinkle with remaining mozzarella cheese.   *Makes 4 servings*

Prep Time: 20 minutes
Cook Time: 10 minutes

hearty bbq beef sandwich

chicken and pasta primavera

1 tablespoon I CAN'T BELIEVE IT'S NOT BUTTER!® Spread
¾ pound boneless, skinless chicken breasts, cut into thin strips
2 cloves garlic, finely chopped
1 cup water
½ cup dry white wine or water
1 package KNORR® Spring Vegetable recipe mix
½ teaspoon freshly ground pepper
8 ounces linguine, cooked and drained
   Grated Parmesan cheese (optional)

- In large skillet, melt I Can't Believe It's Not Butter!® Spread over medium-high heat and cook chicken and garlic, stirring frequently, 5 minutes.

- Stir in water, wine, recipe mix and pepper. Bring to a boil over high heat, stirring constantly. Reduce heat to low and simmer 5 minutes or until chicken is thoroughly cooked.

- Toss chicken mixture with hot linguine. Serve, if desired, with grated cheese. *Makes 6 servings*

Prep Time: 20 minutes
Cook Time: 12 minutes

chicken and pasta primavera

apricot pork chops and dressing

1 package (6 ounces) herb-seasoned stuffing mix
½ cup dried apricots (about 16), cut into quarters
6 bone-in pork chops, ½ inch thick
   Salt and black pepper
6 tablespoons apricot jam
1 bag (16 ounces) frozen green peas
3 cups matchstick carrots*

*Precut matchstick carrots are available in the produce section of large supermarkets.

1. Preheat oven to 450°F. Spray 6 (18×12-inch) sheets heavy-duty foil with nonstick cooking spray. Prepare stuffing mix according to package directions; stir in apricots.

2. Place ½ cup stuffing mixture in center of one sheet of foil. Place 1 pork chop over stuffing mixture, pressing down slightly and shaping stuffing to conform to shape of chop. Sprinkle with salt and pepper. Spread 1 tablespoon apricot jam over pork chop.

3. Place ⅔ cup peas beside pork chop in curve of bone. Arrange ½ cup carrots around outside of chop.

4. Double fold sides and ends of foil to seal packet, leaving head space for heat circulation. Repeat with remaining stuffing mixture, pork chops, salt, pepper, jam and vegetables to make 5 more packets. Place packets on baking sheet.

5. Bake 25 minutes or until pork chops are barely pink in centers and vegetables are tender. Remove from oven. Carefully open one end of each packet to allow steam to escape. Open packets and transfer contents to serving plates. *Makes 6 servings*

apricot pork chop and dressing

fast 'n easy chili

1½ pounds ground beef
  1 envelope LIPTON® RECIPE SECRETS® Onion Soup Mix*
  1 can (15 to 19 ounces) red kidney or black beans, drained
1½ cups water
  1 can (8 ounces) tomato sauce
  4 teaspoons chili powder

Also terrific with LIPTON® RECIPE SECRETS® Onion Mushroom or Beefy Onion Soup Mix.

1. In 12-inch skillet, brown ground beef over medium-high heat; drain.

2. Stir in remaining ingredients. Bring to a boil over high heat. Reduce heat to low and simmer covered, stirring occasionally, 20 minutes. Top hot chili with shredded Cheddar cheese and serve, if desired, over hot cooked rice.

Makes 6 servings

First Alarm Chili: Add 5 teaspoons chili powder.

Second Alarm Chili: Add 2 tablespoons chili powder.

Third Alarm Chili: Add chili powder at your own risk.

quick chicken stew with biscuits

1 can (about 10¾ ounces) cream of roasted chicken soup with savory herbs, undiluted
1 bag (16 ounces) frozen Southwestern or Mexican-style vegetables
1 package (about 10 ounces) PERDUE® SHORT CUTS® Fully Cooked Carved Chicken Breast, Honey Roasted
1 package (8 ounces) shredded Mexican or Monterey Jack cheese (2 cups), divided
1½ cups buttermilk baking mix
  ½ cup milk

Preheat oven to 425°F. In lightly greased 12×8-inch baking dish, combine soup and ½ can water. Stir in vegetables, chicken and 1 cup cheese. Cover and bake 20 minutes. Meanwhile, combine baking mix, remaining 1 cup cheese and milk; stir with fork until all of baking mix is moistened. Spoon baking mix over chicken mixture. Bake 15 to 20 minutes until biscuit topping is golden brown and sauce is hot and bubbly.

Makes 4 to 6 servings

fast 'n easy chili

santa fe fish fillets with mango-cilantro salsa

Nonstick cooking spray
1½ pounds fish fillets (cod, perch or tilapia, about ½ inch thick)
½ package (3 tablespoons) ORTEGA® Taco Seasoning Mix
3 ORTEGA Taco Shells, finely crushed
1 cup ORTEGA Salsa, any variety
½ cup diced mango
2 tablespoons chopped cilantro

PREHEAT oven to 375°F. Cover broiler pan with foil. Spray with cooking spray.

DIP fish fillets in taco seasoning mix, coating both sides; place on foil. Spray coated fillets with cooking spray. Sprinkle with crushed taco shells.

BAKE 15 to 20 minutes until flaky in center.

MICROWAVE salsa on HIGH (100%) 1 minute. Stir in mango and cilantro.

SPOON salsa over fish before serving.   *Makes 4 to 6 servings*

Note: Refrigerated jars of sliced mango can be found in the produce section of most supermarkets.

santa fe fish fillet with mango-cilantro salsa

simply delicious pasta primavera

¼ cup I CAN'T BELIEVE IT'S NOT BUTTER!® Spread
1 envelope LIPTON® RECIPE SECRETS® Vegetable Soup Mix
1½ cups milk
8 ounces linguine or spaghetti, cooked and drained
¼ cup grated Parmesan cheese (about 1 ounce)

1. In medium saucepan, melt spread over medium heat; stir in soup mix and milk. Bring just to a boil over high heat.

2. Reduce heat to low and simmer uncovered, stirring occasionally, 10 minutes or until vegetables are tender. Toss hot linguine with sauce and Parmesan cheese. *Makes 4 servings*

Prep Time: 5 minutes
Cook Time: 12 minutes

turkey tacos

1 tablespoon vegetable oil
1 small onion, sliced
1 small red or green bell pepper, sliced
1 pound boneless, skinless turkey breast, cut into strips
¾ cup water
1 package (1.25 ounces) ORTEGA® Taco Seasoning Mix
2 tablespoons sour cream
1 package ORTEGA Taco Shells, warmed
   Shredded Mexican cheese blend, chopped tomato, shredded lettuce and ORTEGA Taco Sauce

HEAT oil in large skillet over medium-high heat. Add onion and bell pepper; cook, stirring occasionally, for 3 to 4 minutes or until vegetables are tender. Add turkey; cook, stirring occasionally, for 4 to 5 minutes or until turkey is no longer pink.

ADD water and seasoning mix. Heat until thickened, stirring often. Stir in sour cream.

FILL taco shells with turkey mixture. Top with cheese, tomato, lettuce and taco sauce. *Makes 6 servings*

simply delicious pasta primavera

cheddar broccoli quiche

1½ cups milk

3 eggs

1 package KNORR® Leek recipe mix

1 package (10 ounces) frozen chopped broccoli, thawed and drained

1½ cups shredded Cheddar, Swiss or Monterey Jack cheese (about 6 ounces)

1 (9-inch) unbaked or frozen deep-dish pie crust*

If using 9-inch deep-dish frozen prepared pie crust, do not thaw. Preheat oven and cookie sheet. Pour filling into pie crust; bake on cookie sheet.

● Preheat oven to 375°F. In large bowl, with fork, beat milk, eggs and recipe mix until blended. Stir in broccoli and cheese; spoon into pie crust.

● Bake 40 minutes or until knife inserted 1 inch from edge comes out clean. Let stand 10 minutes before serving.   *Makes 6 servings*

Tip: Cheddar Broccoli Quiche accompanied with fresh fruit or cherry tomatoes is perfect for brunch or lunch. Or serve it with a mixed green salad and soup for a hearty dinner.

Prep Time: 10 minutes
Cook Time: 40 minutes

white chicken chili

1 to 2 tablespoons canola oil

1 onion, chopped (about 1 cup)

1 package (about 1¼ pounds) PERDUE® Fresh Ground Chicken, Turkey or Turkey Breast Meat

1 package (about 1¾ ounces) chili seasoning mix

1 can (14½ ounces) reduced-sodium chicken broth

1 can (15 ounces) cannellini or white kidney beans, drained and rinsed

In Dutch oven over medium-high heat, heat oil. Add onion; sauté 2 to 3 minutes or until softened and translucent. Add ground chicken; sauté 5 to 7 minutes or until no longer pink. Add chili mix and stir to combine. Add chicken broth and beans; bring to a boil. Reduce heat to medium-low; simmer 5 to 10 minutes or until all flavors are blended.   *Makes 4 servings*

Prep Time: 10 minutes
Cook Time: 10 to 20 minutes

cheddar broccoli quiche

asian noodles with vegetables and chicken

1 tablespoon vegetable oil

2 cups sliced shiitake or button mushrooms

2 cups fresh snow peas, sliced diagonally in half

2 packages (1.6 ounces each) garlic and vegetable instant rice noodle soup mix

2 cups boiling water

2 packages (about 6 ounces each) refrigerated fully cooked chicken breast strips, cut into pieces

¼ teaspoon red pepper flakes

2 tablespoons fresh lime juice

1 tablespoon soy sauce

2 tablespoons chopped cilantro or sliced green onion

1. Heat oil in large skillet over medium-high heat. Add mushrooms and snow peas; cook 2 to 3 minutes. Remove from skillet.

2. Break up noodles from soup mix. Add noodles, 1 seasoning packet, water, chicken and red pepper flakes to skillet; mix well. Cook over medium-high heat 5 to 7 minutes or until liquid thickens. Stir in reserved vegetables, lime juice and soy sauce. Sprinkle with cilantro. Serve immediately.

Makes 4 servings

quick tip

Originally from Japan, shiitake mushrooms are now cultivated in the United States and other countries. These mushrooms have dark brown caps and tough, woody stems, which are usually trimmed away before cooking. Shiitakes have a firm, meaty texture and rich, smoky flavor.

asian noodles with vegetables and chicken

garlic 'n lemon roast chicken

1 small onion, finely chopped
1 envelope LIPTON® RECIPE SECRETS® Savory Herb with Garlic Soup Mix
2 tablespoons BERTOLLI® Olive Oil
2 tablespoons lemon juice
1 (3½-pound) roasting chicken

1. In large plastic bag or bowl, combine onion and soup mix blended with oil and lemon juice; add chicken. Close bag and shake, or toss in bowl, until chicken is evenly coated. Cover and marinate in refrigerator, turning occasionally, 2 hours.

2. Preheat oven to 350°F. Place chicken and marinade in 13×9-inch baking or roasting pan. Arrange chicken, breast side up; discard bag.

3. Bake uncovered, basting occasionally, 1 hour and 20 minutes or until meat thermometer reaches 180°F. (Insert meat thermometer into thickest part of thigh between breast and thigh; make sure tip does not touch bone.)
Makes 4 servings

beef stroganoff

12 ounces uncooked wide egg noodles
1 can (10¾ ounces) condensed cream of mushroom soup, undiluted
1 cup (8 ounces) sour cream
1 package (1¼ ounces) dry onion soup mix
1½ pounds ground beef
1 cup frozen peas, thawed

1. Cook noodles according to package directions; drain and keep warm.

2. Meanwhile, combine mushroom soup, sour cream and onion soup mix in medium bowl; stir until blended. Brown meat in large skillet over high heat 6 to 8 minutes or until meat is no longer pink, stirring to separate meat. Drain fat. Reduce heat to low. Add soup mixture; stir over low heat until bubbly. Stir in peas; heat through. Serve over noodles.   *Makes 6 servings*

garlic 'n lemon roast chicken

cranberry-onion pork roast

1 boneless pork loin roast (about 2 pounds)
1 can (16 ounces) whole cranberry sauce
1 package (1 ounce) dry onion soup mix

Season roast with salt and black pepper; place over indirect heat on grill. Stir together cranberry sauce and onion soup mix in small microwavable bowl. Heat, covered, in microwave until hot, about 1 minute. Baste roast with cranberry mixture every 10 minutes until roast is done (internal temperature with a meat thermometer is 155° to 160°F), about 30 to 45 minutes. Let roast rest about 5 to 8 minutes before slicing to serve. Heat any leftover basting mixture to boiling; stir and boil for 5 minutes. Serve alongside roast.

Makes 4 to 6 servings

Favorite recipe from **National Pork Board**

spring vegetable quiche

4 eggs
1½ cups milk
1 package (10 ounces) frozen chopped spinach, thawed and squeezed dry
1 cup shredded Swiss cheese (about 4 ounces)
1 package KNORR® Spring Vegetable recipe mix
1 (9-inch) frozen deep-dish pie crust

• Preheat oven and cookie sheet to 350°F.

• In large bowl, with wire whisk, beat eggs lightly. Blend in milk, spinach, cheese and recipe mix. Pour into frozen pie crust.

• Bake on cookie sheet 50 minutes or until knife inserted halfway between center and edge comes out clean.   *Makes about 6 servings*

Prep Time: 10 minutes
Cook Time: 50 minutes

cranberry-onion pork roast

chicken & savory rice

  2 tablespoons butter, divided
  4 boneless skinless chicken breasts (about 1 pound)
  ½ teaspoon black pepper
  ½ teaspoon dried thyme
  1 package (about 7 ounces) chicken-flavored rice and vermicelli mix
  1 cup sliced mushrooms
  ½ cup chopped onion
1¼ cups water
  1 cup apple juice
  1 medium apple, cored and chopped (about 1 cup)
  ¼ cup dried cranberries or currants

1. Melt 1 tablespoon butter in large skillet over medium-high heat. Add chicken; sprinkle with pepper and thyme. Brown chicken on both sides. Remove from skillet; set aside.

2. Melt remaining 1 tablespoon butter in same skillet. Add rice mix, mushrooms and onion; cook and stir over medium heat until mixture is golden brown.

3. Stir in water, apple juice, apple, cranberries and contents of seasoning packet; bring to a boil. Arrange chicken over rice. Reduce heat to medium-low. Cover; simmer 15 to 20 minutes or until chicken is no longer pink in center and rice is tender. Let stand 5 minutes before serving.

Makes 4 servings

Prep Time: 10 minutes
Cook Time: 35 minutes

chicken & savory rice

souper stuffed cheese burgers

1 envelope LIPTON® RECIPE SECRETS® Onion Soup Mix*
2 pounds ground beef
½ cup water
**¾ cup shredded Cheddar, mozzarella or Monterey Jack cheese
    (about 6 ounces)**

*Also terrific with LIPTON® RECIPE SECRETS® Savory Herb with Garlic, Onion Mushroom or Beefy Onion Soup Mix.

1. In large bowl, combine soup mix, ground beef and water; shape into 12 patties.

2. Place 2 tablespoons cheese in center of 6 patties. Top with remaining patties and seal edges tightly.

3. Grill or broil until done. Serve, if desired, on onion poppy seed rolls.

Makes 6 servings

Recipe Tip: To perk up your burgers, serve them on something besides a bun. Try bagels, English muffins, pita bread or even tortillas for a change of pace!

spanish skillet supper

1 tablespoon vegetable oil
1 pound boneless skinless chicken breasts, cut into 1-inch cubes
2 cups hot water
1 package (4.4 ounces) Spanish rice and sauce mix
2 cups BIRDS EYE® frozen Green Peas
    Crushed red pepper flakes

● Heat oil in large skillet over medium-high heat. Add chicken; cook and stir until lightly browned, about 5 minutes.

● Add hot water, rice and sauce mix; bring to boil. Reduce heat to medium-low; simmer, uncovered, 5 minutes.

● Stir in green peas; increase heat to medium-high. Cover and cook 5 minutes or until peas and rice are tender.

● Sprinkle with red pepper flakes.

Makes about 4 servings

souper stuffed cheese burger

super speedy sides

pizza biscuits

2½ cups baking mix
1 cup CABOT® Sour Cream
4 ounces CABOT® Sharp Cheddar, grated (1 cup)
½ cup chopped cooked ham

1. Preheat oven to 400°F.

2. In mixing bowl, combine baking mix, sour cream, cheese and ham; stir together to form soft dough.

3. Turn dough out onto lightly floured work surface and pat into ¾-inch-thick layer. Cut out biscuits with cutter. Place on baking sheet.

4. Bake for 12 to 15 minutes or until golden brown; serve hot.

Makes about 12 biscuits

pizza biscuits

apple pecan stuffing

½ cup (1 stick) butter
1 large onion, chopped
1 large Granny Smith apple, peeled, diced
2½ cups chicken broth
1 package (16 ounces) corn bread stuffing mix
½ cup chopped pecans, toasted

1. Preheat oven to 325°F. Melt butter in large saucepan. Add onion; cook 5 minutes, stirring occasionally. Add apple; cook 1 minute. Add broth; bring to a simmer. Remove from heat; stir in stuffing mix and pecans.

2. If desired, loosely fill cavity of turkey with stuffing just before roasting. Place remaining stuffing in ovenproof casserole. Cover and bake 45 minutes or until hot. (Or, stuffing may be baked at 375°F 30 minutes while turkey is standing.) *Makes 10 to 12 servings*

Note: Stuffing may be prepared up to 1 day before serving (store covered and refrigerated). Let stand at room temperature 30 minutes before baking or stuffing turkey.

easy "baked" beans

2 slices bacon, chopped
2 cans (19 ounces each) red kidney beans and/or cannellini beans, rinsed and drained
1 envelope LIPTON® RECIPE SECRETS® Beefy Onion Soup Mix
1½ cups water
¼ cup ketchup
2 tablespoons firmly packed brown sugar

1. In 3-quart saucepan, cook bacon over medium-high heat until crisp-tender. Stir in beans and cook, stirring frequently, 1 minute.

2. Stir in remaining ingredients. Bring to a boil over high heat.

3. Reduce heat to medium-low and simmer uncovered, 20 minutes or until thickened. *Makes 6 servings*

Prep Time: 10 minutes
Cook Time: 25 minutes

apple pecan stuffing

bayou dirty rice

¼ **pound spicy sausage, crumbled**
½ **medium onion, chopped**
1 **stalk celery, sliced**
1 **package (6 ounces) wild and long grain rice seasoned mix**
1 **can (14½ ounces) DEL MONTE® Stewed Tomatoes - Original Recipe**
½ **green bell pepper, chopped**
¼ **cup chopped fresh parsley**

1. Brown sausage and onion in large skillet over medium-high heat; drain. Add celery, rice and rice seasoning packet; cook and stir 2 minutes.

2. Drain tomatoes, reserving liquid; pour liquid into measuring cup. Add water to measure 1⅓ cups; pour over rice. Add tomatoes; bring to a boil. Cover and cook over low heat 20 minutes. Add bell pepper and parsley.

3. Cover and cook 5 minutes or until rice is tender. Serve with roasted chicken or Cornish game hens. *Makes 4 to 6 servings*

creamed spinach

2 **cups milk**
1 **package KNORR® Leek recipe mix**
1 **bag (16 ounces) frozen chopped spinach**
⅛ **teaspoon ground nutmeg**

• In medium saucepan, combine milk and recipe mix. Bring to a boil over medium heat.

• Add spinach and nutmeg, stirring frequently. Bring to a boil over high heat. Reduce heat to low and simmer, stirring frequently, 5 minutes.

Makes 6 servings

Prep Time: 5 minutes
Cook Time: 10 minutes

bayou dirty rice

super-moist cornbread

1 can (11 ounces) Mexican-style corn, drained
1 package (8½ ounces) corn muffin mix
½ cup HELLMANN'S® or BEST FOODS® Real Mayonnaise
1 egg, slightly beaten

1. Preheat oven to 400°F. Spray 8-inch round cake pan with nonstick cooking spray; set aside.

2. In medium bowl, combine all ingredients until moistened. Spread evenly in prepared pan.

3. Bake 25 minutes or until toothpick inserted into center comes out clean.

Makes 8 servings

Prep Time: 5 minutes
Cook Time: 25 minutes

roasted idaho & sweet potatoes

2 medium all-purpose potatoes, peeled, if desired, and cut into large chunks (about 1 pound)
2 medium sweet potatoes or yams, peeled, if desired, and cut into large chunks (about 1 pound)
¼ cup BERTOLLI® Olive Oil
1 envelope LIPTON® RECIPE SECRETS® Onion Soup Mix

1. Preheat oven to 425°F. In large plastic bag or bowl, combine all ingredients. Close bag and shake, or toss in bowl, until potatoes are evenly coated.

2. In 13×9-inch baking or roasting pan, arrange potatoes; discard bag.

3. Bake uncovered, stirring occasionally, 40 minutes or until potatoes are tender and golden.

Makes 4 servings

super-moist cornbread

grilled mesquite vegetables

2 to 3 tablespoons MRS. DASH® Mesquite Grilling Blend
2 tablespoons olive oil, divided
1 eggplant, trimmed and cut into ½-inch slices
1 zucchini, quartered lengthwise
1 red onion, peeled and halved
2 red bell peppers, cut into large slices
2 green bell peppers, cut into large slices
1 tablespoon balsamic vinegar

Preheat barbecue grill to medium. In large bowl, combine Mrs. Dash®
Mesquite Grilling Blend and 1 tablespoon olive oil. Add vegetables and
toss until well coated. Place vegetables on grill. Cover and cook, turning
vegetables once during cooking, until vegetables are tender and develop
grill marks, about 3 to 4 minutes on each side. Remove vegetables from grill
as soon as they are cooked. Coarsely chop vegetables into ½-inch pieces. Mix
remaining olive oil and balsamic vinegar in large bowl. Add cut vegetables
and toss to coat. Serve at room temperature.   *Makes 6 servings*

holiday wild rice pilaf

2 tablespoons butter or margarine
½ cup chopped onion
½ cup sliced celery
1 can (14½ ounces) low-salt chicken broth
½ cup water
1 package (6 ounces) original flavor long grain and wild rice mix
¾ cup SUN-MAID® Raisins or Goldens & Cherries
⅓ cup coarsely chopped pecans, toasted

MELT butter in medium saucepan or skillet over medium-high heat.

ADD onion and celery; cook 3 minutes, stirring occasionally.

ADD broth, water, rice, contents of seasoning packet and fruit. Bring to
a boil. Reduce heat to medium-low. Cover and simmer 25 minutes or
until liquid is absorbed. Stir in pecans. Serve pilaf as a side dish or use as
stuffing for turkey or chicken.   *Makes 4 to 6 servings (about 4½ cups)*

grilled mesquite vegetables

south-of-the-border rice and beans

1¼ cups water
1 cup ORTEGA® Salsa, any variety
½ package (3 tablespoons) ORTEGA Taco Seasoning Mix
2 teaspoons vegetable oil
2 cups uncooked instant white rice
1 can (about 15 ounces) pinto beans, rinsed and drained
¼ cup chopped cilantro

COMBINE water, salsa, seasoning mix and oil in large saucepan; mix well. Stir in rice and beans; mix well.

BRING to a boil over medium-high heat. Cover; remove from heat. Let stand 5 minutes.

STIR in cilantro.   *Makes 4 servings*

Tip: Serve this side dish with grilled chicken or pork. Brush the meat with oil and sprinkle with extra taco seasoning mix for a flavorful entrée.

souper stuffing

2 packages KNORR® Recipe Classics™ Vegetable or French Onion Recipe Mix
4 cups water
½ cup (1 stick) margarine or butter
1 package (14 to 15 ounces) unseasoned cube stuffing mix

● Preheat oven to 350°F. Lightly grease 3-quart casserole. In large saucepan, combine recipe mix, water and margarine; stirring occasionally, heat to boiling. Remove from heat.

● Stir in stuffing mix just until evenly moistened. Spoon into prepared casserole.

● Bake 30 minutes or until lightly browned and heated through.
                                                   Makes 12 servings

Sausage Stuffing: In step 1, sauté ½ pound crumbled sausage in saucepan before adding water and recipe mix. Reduce margarine to 4 tablespoons.

Prep Time: 10 minutes
Cook Time: 30 minutes

south-of-the-border rice and beans

broccoli casserole with crumb topping

2 slices day-old white bread, coarsely crumbled (about 1¼ cups)
½ cup shredded mozzarella cheese (about 2 ounces)
2 tablespoons chopped fresh parsley (optional)
2 tablespoons BERTOLLI® Olive Oil, divided
1 clove garlic, finely chopped
6 cups broccoli florets and/or cauliflowerets
1 envelope LIPTON® RECIPE SECRETS® Onion Soup Mix
1 cup water
1 large tomato, chopped

1. In small bowl, combine bread crumbs, cheese, parsley, 1 tablespoon oil and garlic; set aside.

2. In 12-inch skillet, heat remaining 1 tablespoon oil over medium heat and cook broccoli, stirring frequently, 2 minutes.

3. Stir in soup mix blended with water. Bring to a boil over high heat. Reduce heat to low and simmer uncovered, stirring occasionally, 8 minutes or until broccoli is almost tender. Add tomato and simmer 2 minutes.

4. Spoon vegetable mixture into 1½-quart casserole; top with bread crumb mixture. Broil 1½ minutes or until crumbs are golden and cheese is melted.

Makes 6 servings

quick tip

Choose firm broccoli stems with tightly packed dark green buds and crisp leaves. Avoid heads that are light green in color with wilted, yellowed leaves, open buds or tiny yellow flowers which indicate overmaturity. Fresh broccoli should be stored unwashed in a plastic bag; it will keep four to five days in the refrigerator.

broccoli casserole with crumb topping

southwestern sausage drop biscuits

    1 pound BOB EVANS® Zesty Hot Roll Sausage
    3 cups all-purpose biscuit baking mix
 1¼ cups (5 ounces) shredded sharp Cheddar cheese
    1 cup seeded diced fresh or drained canned tomatoes
    1 cup chopped green onions
    1 cup milk
   ¼ teaspoon paprika
      Dash cayenne pepper
      Butter (optional)

Preheat oven to 350°F. Crumble and cook sausage in medium skillet until browned. Drain on paper towels. Combine sausage and remaining ingredients except butter in large bowl; mix well. Shape dough into 2-inch balls; place on ungreased baking sheet. Bake 12 minutes or until golden. Serve hot with butter, if desired. Refrigerate leftovers.

Makes about 2 dozen small biscuits

savory skillet broccoli

    1 tablespoon BERTOLLI® Olive Oil
    6 cups fresh broccoli florets *or* 1 pound green beans, trimmed
    1 envelope LIPTON® RECIPE SECRETS® Golden Onion Soup Mix*
 1½ cups water

*Also terrific with LIPTON® RECIPE SECRETS® Onion Mushroom Soup Mix.

1. In 12-inch skillet, heat olive oil over medium-high heat and cook broccoli, stirring occasionally, 2 minutes.

2. Stir in soup mix blended with water. Bring to a boil over high heat.

3. Reduce heat to medium-low and simmer covered, 6 minutes or until broccoli is tender.

Makes 4 servings

Prep Time: 5 minutes
Cook Time: 10 minutes

southwestern sausage drop biscuits

fiesta-style roasted vegetables

1 can (4 ounces) ORTEGA® Diced Green Chiles
3 tablespoons vinegar
2 tablespoons vegetable oil
1 package (1.25 ounces) ORTEGA Taco Seasoning Mix
1 small red bell pepper, cut into strips
1 medium zucchini, cut into ½-inch slices
1 small sweet potato, peeled, halved and cut into ⅛-inch slices
1 small red onion, cut into wedges
  Nonstick cooking spray

COMBINE chiles, vinegar, oil and seasoning mix in large bowl; mix well. Add red pepper, zucchini, sweet potato and onion; toss gently to coat. Let stand at room temperature 15 minutes to marinate.

PREHEAT oven to 450°F. Cover 15×10-inch baking pan with foil and spray with cooking spray.

REMOVE vegetables from marinade with spoon; place on prepared pan.

BAKE 20 to 25 minutes until tender and browned, stirring once.

Makes 4 servings

Tip: Substitute yellow squash for the zucchini, if preferred.

scalloped garlic potatoes

3 medium all-purpose potatoes, peeled and thinly sliced (about 1½ pounds)
1 envelope LIPTON® RECIPE SECRETS® Savory Herb with Garlic Soup Mix
1 cup (½ pint) whipping or heavy cream
½ cup water

1. Preheat oven to 375°F. In lightly greased 2-quart shallow baking dish, arrange potatoes. In medium bowl, blend remaining ingredients; pour over potatoes.

2. Bake, uncovered, 45 minutes or until potatoes are tender.

Makes 4 servings

acknowledgments

The publisher would like to thank the companies and organizations listed below for the use of their recipes and photographs in this publication.

ACH Food Companies, Inc.

Allen Canning Company

American Lamb Council

Birds Eye Foods

Bob Evans®

Cabot® Creamery Cooperative

Cherry Marketing Institute

Del Monte Corporation

The Golden Grain Company®

Hormel Foods, LLC

Mrs. Dash®

National Pork Board

Ortega®, A Division of B&G Foods, Inc.

Perdue Farms Incorporated

Reckitt Benckiser Inc.

Sonoma® Dried Tomatoes

Sun•Maid® Growers of California

Unilever

Veg•All®

metric conversion chart

VOLUME MEASUREMENTS (dry)

$1/8$ teaspoon = 0.5 mL
$1/4$ teaspoon = 1 mL
$1/2$ teaspoon = 2 mL
$3/4$ teaspoon = 4 mL
1 teaspoon = 5 mL
1 tablespoon = 15 mL
2 tablespoons = 30 mL
$1/4$ cup = 60 mL
$1/3$ cup = 75 mL
$1/2$ cup = 125 mL
$2/3$ cup = 150 mL
$3/4$ cup = 175 mL
1 cup = 250 mL
2 cups = 1 pint = 500 mL
3 cups = 750 mL
4 cups = 1 quart = 1 L

VOLUME MEASUREMENTS (fluid)

1 fluid ounce (2 tablespoons) = 30 mL
4 fluid ounces ($1/2$ cup) = 125 mL
8 fluid ounces (1 cup) = 250 mL
12 fluid ounces ($1 1/2$ cups) = 375 mL
16 fluid ounces (2 cups) = 500 mL

WEIGHTS (mass)

$1/2$ ounce = 15 g
1 ounce = 30 g
3 ounces = 90 g
4 ounces = 120 g
8 ounces = 225 g
10 ounces = 285 g
12 ounces = 360 g
16 ounces = 1 pound = 450 g

DIMENSIONS

$1/16$ inch = 2 mm
$1/8$ inch = 3 mm
$1/4$ inch = 6 mm
$1/2$ inch = 1.5 cm
$3/4$ inch = 2 cm
1 inch = 2.5 cm

OVEN TEMPERATURES

250°F = 120°C
275°F = 140°C
300°F = 150°C
325°F = 160°C
350°F = 180°C
375°F = 190°C
400°F = 200°C
425°F = 220°C
450°F = 230°C

BAKING PAN SIZES

Utensil	Size in Inches/Quarts	Metric Volume	Size in Centimeters
Baking or Cake Pan (square or rectangular)	8×8×2	2 L	20×20×5
	9×9×2	2.5 L	23×23×5
	12×8×2	3 L	30×20×5
	13×9×2	3.5 L	33×23×5
Loaf Pan	8×4×3	1.5 L	20×10×7
	9×5×3	2 L	23×13×7
Round Layer Cake Pan	8×1½	1.2 L	20×4
	9×1½	1.5 L	23×4
Pie Plate	8×1¼	750 mL	20×3
	9×1¼	1 L	23×3
Baking Dish or Casserole	1 quart	1 L	—
	1½ quart	1.5 L	—
	2 quart	2 L	—